Islands in the Sky

Also by David Meuel

STAGE PLAYS
The End of All That
Deliverance and Destiny

NON-FICTION
Building Strategic Relationships (co-author)

ISLANDS IN THE SKY

POEMS
by
DAVID MEUEL

PURISIMA CREEK PRESS
Palo Alto, California

Acknowledgements

The poems in this book first appeared, sometimes in different versions, in the following periodicals:

Acorn: "Morning at the Vernal Falls Bridge," "Vogelsang"
Bellowing Ark: "First Born," "Freshly Cut Roses"
Black Fly Review: "The High Country," "On Black Point," "The Plates," "The Vietnam War Memorial"
Caesura: "Lake Tenaya"
Convolvus: "The Stakeout"
Coracle: "The Narrows"
Dallas Review: "Finishing Touches," The September Snow Plant"
Dominion Review: "Tired of the Same Old Job?"
Echoes: "A Moment in Passing"
Hidden Springs Review: "Descending"
Kings Review: "The Rising Tide"
Laureate Letter: "The Beach at Dusk"
Lynx Eye: "Dead Horse Point"
Northwest Literary Forum: "The Flowers in My Grandmother's Books"
On Target: "Ode to My Creditors"
Orphic Lute: "Chance Meeting in a Department Store," "Moonless Night on Thousand Island Lake"
Pearl: "After You Left," "Personality," "Ten Years Together"
Poetic Page: "As Mom Drove"
Poetry Motel: "The Green Lantern"
Poets On: "Biodegradable"
Santa Clara Review: "The Fire Fall"
Tomorrow: "A Valentine's Day Wish"
Tule Review: "Dad's Giggle"
Wildfire: "The Outpouring"
Writers Gazette: "The Desert's Silence"

"The Back Country" has also appeared in the book, *In Our Fifties: Voices of Men and Women Reinventing Their Lives,* by William Bergquist Elinor Miller Greenberg, and G. Alan Klaum (Jossey-Bass, Inc., 1993). In addition, "The Back Country," "A Moment in Passing," and "The September Snow Plant" received recognition in the Biennial Poetry Competition sponsored by the Villa Montalvo Center for the Arts in Saratoga, California. "Descending" was a winner in a poetry contest sponsored by *Hidden Springs Review* in Los Angeles.

Finally, I would like to thank Bob Ferrando, Scotty Martinson, and Peter Nelson for their help in developing this manuscript.

© 1997 by David Meuel
ISBN 0-9658374-0-8 (pbk)
Printed in U.S.A.

For Barbara

Contents

III. The Desert's Long Dull Stare

IV. We Talk in Touches Now

Life is so short
we must move very slowly.

—Thai saying

I

I Shadow Dad

The High Country

When it was time
to climb the stairs that night,
Dad went first, like he always did.
He put his right hand on the railing,
then dragged each stone foot up
in slow and strained, supremely careful moves.
And together we inched our way along.

As we climbed, I thought
of the pack trips we used to take.
He was in front then, too,
his strong, stocky legs
guiding us over smooth white passes
that held the sky like open hands.
He was in front then, too.

But now his legs were thin and weak,
dry sticks still clinging to the ancient oak.
Now his high country
was a room one story up
where craggy ledges hung
in wooden picture frames
and plants and flowers grew
in round red earthen pots.

So, to the room we climbed.
And, as we did, I saw in his eyes
an evening calm.
This was not a time for tears, they said,
simply a time for less.

The Flowers
in My Grandmother's Books

Brittle bright
in their letter-lined tombs,
they gaze
into my wide young eyes
and whisper in a language
as elusive as rainbows.

Are they asking me
to turn the page
and let them rest in peace?

Or is it to pause
and enjoy their beauty
as I would a butterfly's
in its presentation case?

Or is their message hers?
Had she placed them there
to beckon me back,
back to that
dinosaur distant day
when they—and she—
sipped the same
restless, rollicking air?

First Born

I unwrap you just enough
to free your arms.
You raise them both,
make two fists,
and strike the air:
a boxer
conducting an orchestra.

The Great Depression

I.

My father's father,
who came from money
then lost most of it in the Crash of '29,
spent much of the Great Depression
sitting in his easy chair,
smoking cigarettes,
and listening to records of operas
that featured the great Caruso.
He wanted to work, he said,
and he did hold jobs from time to time.
But nothing ever seemed to last,
and he always returned to his tenor
with the wide, transcendent voice.

One evening, my grandmother,
who now worked long days
in a cramped little sewing shop,
came home to hear Caruso sing
with added strength and clarity.
Was it a new record?
she asked herself as she opened the door,
wondering how they could ever pay for it.
No,
it was a new phonograph,
he told her,
the best one in the music store.

II.

My father's father
did not survive the Great Depression.
He died of a heart attack, I'm told,
well before his time.
And, because the relatives preferred to talk
about my uncomplaining grandmother,
I know little more about him.
I don't know which his favorite operas were.
Or why jobs were hard for him to keep.
Or how he felt when my grandmother
phoned the music store,
told the manager of their circumstances,
and had the phonograph returned.

But, I sometimes think about that room,
where, two decades later,
I would listen to little boy tunes
on my little boy's record player.
I think about the cigarette smoke
mixing easily
with the brilliant afternoon light,
coating everything he saw
with a shimmering silvery haze.
I think about Caruso's voice
drowning out
the clinking bottles of the milkman
and grinding groans of passing cars.

And I think about him,
still as buried bones,
moving only to lift
or lower his cigarette,
his young, old man's body
sinking deeper,
deeper into that easy
chair.

As Mom Drove

Year after year
we rode along,
lofty Munchkin dignitaries
who barely saw
the perfect gesture
being made each day
on our behalf.

Dad's Giggle

Dad called it
his giggle,
that odd
emotional choke
that first appeared
after the disease
attacked his brain.
But it wasn't
a giggle at all.
It was his
peculiar cry.
A cry
without tears.
A dry cry.
Still, a cry for all
that saddened
or inspired him.

In this respect alone,
infirmity
had set him free.

The Stakeout

I'm being watched—and followed,
shadowed like a suspect in a crime.

The gumshoe is my son, all of seven
and sticking like a sweating shirt.

He studies how I toss a ball
and wield a dinner knife.

He asks me why I watch the news
and steals my favorite turns of phrase.

I'm overwhelmed, but, as he lurks,
another shadow slouches near.

He wonders why I'm such a bore
and chides my choices, all of them.

He damns the day when blood bound us
like feuding tigers in a cage.

My father held one like him tight.

So, once again, I shadow Dad.

The Last Raggedy Ann

I.

She sits upon a dresser
in a small well-tended room
in my younger sister's home:
a life companion
with a weathered smile,
a head of dulling red yarn hair,
and here and there
a slowly decomposing stitch.

II.

Seeing her again, I remember
another small, well-tended room
and a moment
nearly forty years ago.
Our mother's mother,
the last of the grandparents,
wrinkled and bent
and near the end of a long life,
sits before
a pedal-driven sewing machine.
To her left lay bright red yarn,
assorted threads, and patterns
for the doll's body and the dress.
To her right rest clumps of foam
she'll mold into heart and soul.
I remember how fast

this frail woman works:
her fingers, her feet,
so clever, so decisive.
She'd have it done in no time,
this newest Ann
for her newest granddaughter.

III.

Then, as this thread
of memory frays
like threads
upon this aging Ann,
I see her as she is
and perhaps
was always meant to be:
the little left
from the little shared
in the needle's eye of time
we three were all allowed;
a heart and soul preserved
in yarn, in fabric, and in foam.

Vogelsang

(Yosemite, 1969)

You know that it's not
the top of the world,
this tundra
high above the trees.
Still, we swore
that the creek beside us
flowed
straight into the sky.

Dad liked it best
at dusk,
when the melting sun
splashed pink champagne
across the long-faced
domes and cliffs.
"Alpenglow,"
he'd call it.

But that night,
he didn't call it anything.
He simply sat
upon a stump of rock
and sipped
the deepening colors
along with his after-dinner cup:
his dark eyes
married to the ebbing light;
his cold ears
warmed by its silent chant.

The Plates

After they practiced with the choir, my grandfather
would walk the soprano home to the enormous house
with the rolling lawns and gather her like gold dust
in his arms. Soon, he moved from the house where
his wife and children lived. But he came back once,
when no one was there. And he left with every piece
of furniture and china and art that suited him, even a
pair of antique serving plates he had promised to his
daughter.

The trouble is that, at thirteen, this daughter had
known only other parts of him: the wide smile and
the cadenced voice, his generous praise for her work
in school, and the soaring solos he sang at church.
She had not heard about the soprano or the women
who preceded her or how cleverly he would craft a
way around the alimony later on. The trouble is that
he lives inside his daughter still, his voice hearty and
round and full of song, but silent always on the
subject of the plates.

At the Funeral Mass

"What's in the box?" he blurts,
quick as an auctioneer.

"It's your Great Aunt Cecilia,"
his mother says.
"We all loved her very much."

"Then why did you put her in a box?"

So, she strokes
the wild blossoms of his head
and labors for words he can hold
as tightly as the action figures
in his hands. But every time
she answers one question
he lobs out another
that confounds her
like a slippery curve.

Finally, she asks him to be quiet
and play. And, for a while, he does.
With eyes that gleam
like the church wall glass,
he watches his action figures
battle to the death.

One November Night

Dad turned the headlights off.
Then the engine.
Then he squeezed his keys tight,
tight against the thick walls of his palm.
"Your grandma is very sick,"
he told my brother and me.

For a moment, we just sat,
three stiff jackets
in the still station wagon
on the driveway
simmering with shadows.

But then he tried to talk again,
tried to say
that something big as boulders
was crashing down
on our little pebble of experience.

A Moment in Passing

When I saw Dad coming back
from his walk, I listened.
Yes, I could hear them now,
the tired soles that scratched
the pavement like sandpaper skins.
And, as he inched closer,
I thought about all the rest
that time was taking from him,
not just the powers to do
but also the cravings to know.

Beside me at the door, my son
tugged fiercely at my pants.
His outing was what mattered now.
And, as I nodded yes,
I watched his irked impatient eyes
turn into sparkling lakes.
He let me go. And out he shot,
his scuffed white Keds
doubling as his launching pads.

Then, when these two travelers
passed each other on the path,
they paused just long enough
to share a single knowing smile.
And, in that brief eternity,
I framed them in my mind:
outgoing and incoming; .
at opposite ends of the journey
but, for a moment, together.

II

This River Gallops

Impressions of the Canyonlands

(Eastern Utah)

Dead Horse Point

Cold as December bones,
we stand in the dim
blowing warm breath into cupped hands.
The sun is about to rise.
And resting on our chests and tripods
are cameras, cameras,
all poised to pounce
on the first drop of light
as it squirts out
from the eastern peaks
and pours, like atomic syrup,
over this wide, bewildering world
of canyons and buttes
and red splintered rocks.

I check my camera yet again,
anxious to frame immensity in four by six
while knowing
that next week's snapshots
can never be more
than crumbs left over
from the enormous meal
we are about to consume.
Still, they are crumbs I crave,
tiny specks of crust I'll use
to try to recreate the feast.

The Confluence

The guidebook says
that this is where they merge:
these two great rivers,
the Colorado and the Green.

But shoved together is the case,
in a marriage arranged
by stern canyon walls
that press like unrelenting family heads.

Neither much appreciates it, either.
One khaki green,
the other mustard beige,
each stays on its side of the bed.

And in a touchy truce
they flow,
united without uniting,
a consummation unfulfilled.

The Desert's Silence

So clear and deep and calm,
it calls to me from everywhere.

On Black Point

Along the neighboring beach
the waves submit
like obedient dying men:
whitening, quieting,
slowing, thinning,
limping up cold sand
only as far
as decorum decrees.
But here,
against this cowled
executioner of a
rock, the waves
scream out
before they die.
They howl and hiss
and smash and soar.
They strike the sky
with glittering fists,
their knuckles

splintering
into spray.

Still Life

In the middle of a step
along a path
that ran beside
a gathering
of great slouching oaks,
I saw
no branches swaying,
no lizards lurking,
no blades of grass
stroked by
the nimble fingers
of the wind.
So, I stopped, too.

Then, in the middle
of a breath,
I heard
no squirrels skittering,
no waters wandering,
no twigs popping
beneath my boots.
So, I stopped, too.

And the moment held,
the forest asking
whether I wanted to stay
and watch
this pause dissolve
or instead break first,
taking it with me
on my way.

After the Winter Rain

Pillars of fog
drift upward
from the solemn hills.

Are they reaching
for the clouds
that left them behind?

Half Dome

(Looking over from Glacier Point, Yosemite)

Within this vast, granite drama,
it is the dome that dominates.
So round and regular
on the side and in back,
its front—sliced by an ancient glacier—
is abruptly flat,
like a face stripped
of every feature, crease, and bump.

As many before me have done,
I consider the dome's other half:
the part smashed
into a million meaningless pieces
by a million merciless years.
And I wonder what it all
would have looked like
new and uncut and whole?

Oddly, it seems less,
since the fragment captivates
more fully than the whole could ever do.
As a fragment, it is like no other.
As a fragment, it is more itself.
As a fragment, it is
whole.

The Dolphins

(Near the Channel Islands, California)

I blinked,
and there they were,
dozens and scores of them
inviting us
to share a dance
upon a floor
of bright, slapping sea.
Following their lead,
our boat stepped right,
then left, then right again.
Guiding us stride for stride,
they sprang and darted and dove
in chorus lines
of two and three and four.
And together,
we twirled the sea
around the sun.

The September Snow Plant

How out of place it was,
this bright red shoot
standing in this pool
of High Sierra dust.
How lost in time it had become.

It was, after all, a winter life,
conceived like a butterfly
in a womb of white
and, like a butterfly, born to die
soon after that womb dissolved.

But it remained, even as
the ground that fed it
dried and cracked and came apart.
It remained, never knowing
how short its life was meant to be.

The Rising Tide

The silver apron closes in
to claim his castle in the sand.

First, it licks his feet,
and he giggles in surprise.

Then it tears into his moat,
and he moves to dig a deeper one.

Finally, it batters his towers and walls,
and only then does he understand

its power

and indifference.

The Narrows

(Zion Canyon, Utah)

The trail flanks the river
for about a mile, or until
the tall canyon walls
close in upon the land.
After this, the river
becomes our trail.
With wading shoes
and walking sticks
we slice through murky pools
and gently swelling rapids.
We do not know
what we are after.
We only know
that it must be waiting
around the next
dark, alluring bend.

Bear Gulch

Wandering
like the first scent of spring
through unfolding forests,
redwood to oak to pine,
then up
to a long meadow
that dissolves,
like a dream scene,
into the hazy hills nearby,
this trail is different

every time.

Times of Day

Morning at the Vernal Falls Bridge
(Yosemite)

Its waters pound past
like wild, snorting stallions.
This river gallops.

The Neighbor's Garden, Early Afternoon

Gulping down
the summer sun,
the weeds
can barely remember
the flowers
they'd strangled in the spring.

Late Afternoon at Delicate Arch

(Eastern Utah)

Beauty that never thinks
about being beautiful.

The Beach at Dusk

Skies like gray wolves
sulk over blackberry seas.

Flying West

I watch the sun disappear
behind one moping slope of mountains
only to return, hovering,
like a proud glowing skull,
over the next.

After two such resurrections, I ask
how much longer
this day can sneak a life, can
cheat
the pale moon of death.

The Fire Fall

(Yosemite, 1872–1968)

One night
some fiery embers fell
from a High Sierra point.
To those nearby
it was just a spill,
a part of the campfire
that slipped away.
But to those below
it was a red-orange
ribbon unraveling
down a high
black granite wall:
a glowing river flowing
for nearly half a mile.

Soon the spill
became the fire dance
that played for more
than ninety years:
the dance that was,
like every work
of art and life,
an accident that took.

Moonless Night
on Thousand Island Lake

The moon is off tonight,
taking a break
from these ebony waters
and goblin pines.
As I look up,
I enjoy its absence,
for without it
the true lamps of night
leap out
like fierce cold fires.
Tonight, they don't
just speck the sky,
they smother it
with electric sauce.
Tonight, they even
touch the earth,
stroking the lake top
like fireflies
learning to swim.

Coyote Lullaby

(Lake Yellowstone, Wyoming)

It carried like a fist of wind,
that rolling melancholy moan,
down from the blue-black hills
and through the shivering pines
and into my edgy ears. It bit
with sharp suggestive teeth
that cut as deep as dinner knives.

But, the more I settled to this sound,
the way it rose and softly fell,
the way it lingered like a sigh,
the way it vanished then resumed,
I felt the calming pulse of melody.
"Welcome home," my wild host
was telling me. "Now, go to sleep."

III

The Desert's Long Dull Stare

The Green Lantern
(A Brothel in Ely, Nevada)

It's not a house, really.
Just four bruised trailers
crammed inside a chain link fence
along a road that calls itself
"The Loneliest Highway in America."
To the north, rust red rocks,
gnarled like old fingers,
endure the endless stabbing of the wind.
To the south, filthy crows
scan their dusty plates
for mice that fell
sometime in the night.
To the west, there is just
the desert's long dull stare.

It's not a house, really.
More of a place
where professional smiles
work hard
to hide primordial fears.
Where love appears
merely as mirage.
Where defeat finds company
beside the sun-bleached bones
of long-forgotten mice and crows.

Cursed by a Gypsy Woman

(Near the Baptistry, Florence)

So, this is what it's like, I thought
as she stomped away,
seething with a jilted lover's rage.
A moment ago,
this wire-thin woman
in gritty gray clothes
had pinned me tight against a wall,
her open palm
a knife against my chest,
demanding money.
When I refused,
she raised her hand,
delivering a strange, solemn gesture
and, laced with spurts of spittle,
a few dark words
mythic
in their incomprehensibility.
Now, she was gone,
dipping her hook
into a new stream of tourists
just entering the square.
And now I had been damned for life

or at least
until I give her money.

Lake Tenaya

(Yosemite, 1851)

They were not explorers,
the first white men to visit this place.
They were collectors,
soldiers come to take
the remnants of a mountain tribe
to a guarded lowland camp,
a prison under the stars.

But, before their chief was led away
with a rifle pointed at his head,
one of the collectors came to him
to say they'd all agreed
to name this lake Tenaya, after him.

It was an honor
the chief did not understand,
a monument in payment for a home.
Still, it was an honor from an enemy,
a proof that eyes can see
even after hate has sewn them shut.

Two People I'll Never Know

I saw them clearly in
the wilting light on
the cracking pavement in
front of an apartment house
whose pink walls peeled
like sunburnt skin:
a man and a woman,
both about thirty,
shouting at each other
as he slammed the last
of several cardboard boxes
into the trunk
of a tired Mercury.
She wanted him out.
And he couldn't
wait to leave.
She blamed him
for her misery.
And he blamed her
for his.
He closed the trunk,
lit a cigarette,
and, swaggering over
to the driver's door, said:
"With any luck,
we'll never
see each other again.

As he drove off,
she let out a "Fuck you!"
so loud
it slapped like thunder
on unbending air.
After this, she noticed me
and three other people
who had stopped nearby,
her face
startled at first
then ripening plum red.
Finally, she walked up
some stained concrete stairs
to an open door
and a boy in diapers,
her head as low
as a blossom
on a dying rose.

One Friday Morning

She was a brick
of a nun, my
eighth-grade teacher,
a stiff face
on a wall of starch
who could swing a yardstick
quick as a Saracen's sword.

That morning, she was
telling us about gerunds
when someone outside
motioned her to the door.
She listened to an anxious
whisper, drew back
slightly, then returned to us.
"The President has been shot,"
she said, "in Dallas."
She paused, pushing
the next words through like
straggling students into class.
"They think he's
dead."

She didn't ask us to pray, at least
not then. She just stood,
her grammar book
quivering in her hand,
her face
collapsing into crevices,
and these
filling with forbidden tears.

Freshly Cut Roses

He slips the lanky stems
into the lonely vase
that stands in vigil as she lies,
a case of ticking organs
deep in a wakeless sleep.

No, her eyes will not caress
these delicate buds, nor her
nostrils catch their frisky perfume.
But, as his weary eyes confirm,
that's not what matters anymore.

He had filled her arms with buds
during all their years and years.
And soon he will place them
on the wild blades of grass
that will be her blanket, too.

So, why not now as well?
Now, as the gift that once
charged her eyes with light
becomes the tribute
that brings him blessed peace.

The Vietnam War Memorial

(Washington, D.C.)

It's a wall, nothing more,
half-buried and black,
blanketed with names.
But, as I walk down its sloping path,
it deepens,
its names filling to my knees,
then waist, then eyes,
then beyond my highest leaping reach.

On my way, I pass others
who hold candles
or bow their heads to wreaths
or run their fingers lightly
over the chiseled contours
of familiar words.
Along with them,
I bathe in names.

At the News Stands

The leaning man
with zombie eyes
parks his pushcart home
beside the woman
who longs for him
from the cover
of the swingers' guide.

Longings

As they share their tiny cubicle, he
thinks about the world that hides
beneath the pale,
loose-fitting clothes she wears.

What would it be like, he wonders,
to see the breasts that give her blouses
their delicate dome-like shape?
To scoop them up and savor them,
soft mounds of living gelatin?
To feel her nipples tighten
to the tickle of his tongue?

What would it be like, he wonders,
to see the tops of legs
that vanish like daydreams
beneath her skirts?
To hold the dark place that joins those legs
and feel a thaw as splendid as spring?
To enter that place fully, wildly,
with no thoughts of summer or winter
or of fall?

Ode to My Creditors

Your correspondences arrive
as often as new gray hairs,
as promptly as the executioner.
They stare out from the mail slot
like foundling cobras
hankering for my hand.

I bury them deep
in the cavernous catacombs of my desk.
But, as each molasses day proceeds,
I hear them moan in ghostly chorus:
"Pay us. Pay us. Pay us. Pay us."

Finally, when I have no more reprieves,
I grab the pile by the neck,
sink into the quicksand
of my easy chair,
and savor everything you write
like sips of vintage cyanide.

How can I ever repay you
for this endless shower of attention?
Frankly, I haven't a clue.
So, I suppose I must remain
forever in your debt.

A Valentine's Day Wish

Let's cancel Valentine's,
This Barbie doll of days.
Let's serve it to the cat
On tasty mouse filets.

Let's stew it in black oil
Then pull its limbs apart.
Let's drive a pointed stake
Right through its Hallmark heart.

So, there you have it love,
My final Valentine—
Not one more stupid Cupid card
To tell you that you're mine.

Personality

It used to be
that people wanted
to *have* personalities.
Now, they want
to *be* personalities.
And the good news
for each of them is that,
to *be* one,
there's no need
to *have* one.

Returning
to My Old Grammar School

It's true
what they say
about everything
being smaller
when you go back.
That's because
I was smaller then,
myself.
Which made
the blackboards
higher,
the yard sticks
longer,
the yard fights
scarier,
and every one of those
incredibly white-skinned
Sisters of Mercy
bigger.
I'm happy
they've all
shrunk
since then.
But I'd be
happier
if they'd all just
disappear.

An Old Man Stands and Walks

His body opens
like a rusty pocketknife.
Stone shoes
house his feet.

Tired of the Same Old Job?

Then consider a career in poetry.

We're POETEK, an acknowledged leader
in the burgeoning American poetry industry.
We excel in all the proven forms:
historical, pastoral, tragical, and lyrical.
And, if that's not your style, we're also
committed to producing the daring,
irreverent, and no-holds-barred.

We're looking for energetic self-starters,
people who can do as well as dream,
people, perhaps, like you.
We have immediate openings for poets
in our Heroic Couplet, Epic,
and Horatian Ode divisions.
And, to meet exploding customer demand,
we'll soon be staffing up
in our industry-leading Alienation Division.

We'll start you out at $90K,
review your salary every six months,
and give you a great benefits package.
If that isn't enough, we'll set you up
in your own office

with your own expense account
and your own company car.

Keats only dreamed
of soaring with his nightingale.
You *can* soar with us!

POETEK, an equal opportunity employer.

With Calm Authority

In the summer of 1556, as part of Queen Mary's efforts to rid England of Protestants, officials tied one of them, a pregnant woman from Guernsey, to a stake in the middle of town. After a priest gave her his blessing, the officials set fire to the bundles of sticks beneath her. Until this point, all was routine for the bailiff, who had supervised many such events that year. But then, the growing heat of the flames caused the woman's child, a boy, to slip from her womb and onto a burning bundle of sticks. Quickly, an onlooker pulled the boy out and pleaded for its life. With no precedent to guide him, the bailiff hesitated. But, after a moment in prayer, he calmly concluded that, since the baby had been in his mother's womb when she was condemned, it should be burned as well.

Exactly 283 Protestants were put to death for heresy during Queen Mary's eventful four-year reign. I am not sure if this counted as one or two.

When I Think about Revenge Being Self-Destructive

I think about
the sixteenth-century French lawyer
whose wife
served her country
as the king's mistress.
Feeling slighted,
to say the least,
the lawyer made a special point
of getting syphilis
so
he could give it to his wife
so
she could pass it on to the king.

"That'll fix them,"
he must have thought.

Biodegradable

Here's what to do
with what's left of me.
First,
don't stand on ceremony.
And second,
don't do anything
that involves people.
You know
how I hate gatherings,
especially ones
where all eyes
are on me.
Instead,
just plop me down
on a lonely beach
at low tide.
And then
go to a movie.

You needn't worry.
I won't say
an unkind word
about you.
I'll just lie there
taking in the sun
with the starfish
and the kelp

and the other
washed-up things.
Together we'll wait
for the tide to rise,
rinse us off,
and suck us up.

IV

We Talk in Touches Now

After You Left

After you left, your bags
packed tight, I kept
the apartment as it was: the sexy
painting you'd picked out
forever breathless near the bed,
the photographs of you
and us perpetually
beaming from the shelves.

After you left, your dark eyes
dry, I stayed and
dusted photographs
and, every now and then,
would swear I smelled your
sweet swirling hair on
the empty pillow next to me.

After you left, I never
thought that one quiet night
I'd slice up every
hint of you and stuff
the pieces in the trash on
top of greasy chicken bones.

Slowly, It Happens

I puddle my palm
with oil
that fills the room
with cedar trees.

I spread this oil
up and out,
wide as eagles' wings
across your back.

Then,
with thumbs like oars,
I dip and probe and press
and dip again.

Slowly, it happens:

the tight knots loosening,
easing, surrendering;

your body
ebbing with the tide;

your daydreams
drifting into dance.

The Outpouring

It's
the wetness I like.

The way
your pores give birth
to glittering salty beads
that sprout
about your forehead
and run
down your cheeks,
tiny, clinging waterfalls.

The way
their adhesive
yields
as I unwrap you, each
part of your blouse
peeling
like sections of a moist
tomato skin.

The way more beads
grease
our kissing bellies,
letting them slap and
slide like
rapids on rocks in
a river pounding
its path to the sea.

Gatherings

Dreams are the only afterlife we know;...
—Linda Pastan

"I had a dream about my mother,"
she tells me as we make the bed
this morning. "You were in it, too."

We come together often in her mind,
the mother who died
and the husband who came later.

And, while we meet, she listens,
as voices that can never touch
surround her in a tight embrace.

Descending

Let me take my tongue
from your mouth,
easing it out
over the red rolling
waves of your lips.
Then, let me
give it back to you,
gliding it
down
into the salty
wet canyon
between your
stiffening peaks,
down
across the tight
trembling plain
that crests and falls
with quickening pace,
down
to the swelling spring
that calls
for its caress.

Badwater

(Death Valley, California)

I.

So, when she
and her husband
could only manage a delicate distance,
she brought men home,
licked off their clothes,
and swarmed them on the living room rug.
All this
as her husband slept upstairs
in a bed that had once been good to him.
All this
as she imagined him waking, hearing her, listening,
her nipples leaping at the thought.

Her story comes back
as I sit beside this sullen pool of brine
at the edge of this scorched salt wilderness,
as I look high up a mountain
to a sign marked SEA LEVEL,
as I take in the view
from the lowest place in the western world.
In her own way,
she had been here many times.

II.

Along the salt floor, her back and shoulders form,
white with slow curves
just as they were

on all those liquid afternoons
when the world beyond her thirsty sheets
had simply ceased to be.

Her husband
was her ex by then.
And those who had followed him,
and would follow still,
mere phantoms in the sinking evening light.
I would be a phantom soon, myself.
And soon transitions would accelerate,
all wild stroking standardized,
all phantoms blurring into one.

III.

Now, there's just a desert here,
here at the bottom of the western world.
No back or shoulders from another time.
No blind tornado spinning in the loins.
Just desolation of a geologic kind
and brittle memories stirring
in a silent
stinging breeze.

I was, she often said,
the only man she never had to fake it with.
And, as long as I could hear her heightened moans,
I never thought
to disagree.

Chance Meeting
in a Department Store

As our words recalled
those years apart,
my eyes retraced
the edges of her lips:
lips that once
had coiled my body at the touch;
lips I never
wanted to touch again.

Ten Years Together

I wake to the wet of your
tongue licking me long. When
I am ready, you climb me,
your shoulders hunched above
your strained and standing arms,
your nipples hovering
like bulging alien eyes.

Later, as the cool air
glides our glistening bellies,
you ask: "How many times
has it been? A thousand? More?"
I tell you I don't know, either,
and you nod motionlessly,
nesting your cheek against my chest.

Soon, your breathing slows
and deepens. You slip from me,
sliding down to the sweating sheet.
And, just before I blanket us,
I see you as you were a thousand
times ago—your legs are shy,
yet they open wide for me.

Awakened at Three A.M.

I.

The bedcovers
are on the move again,
slipping away
like the last brown leaves
from bare November trees.
Once again,
you wrap them tightly
around you as you sleep.
And, as always,
you do it with such ease
and grace
and subtlety
that I am reminded
of great art.
                    What now? I ask.
Do I boldy tug,
destroying
your cozy cocoon
in one swift,
decisive stroke?
Do I wake you
and ask
for a fair
and gracious compromise?
Or do I simply
let you sleep
while I search my kingdom
for another covering?

II.

Then, when I turn
to your side of the bed
and find
only a great flat land
of moonlit quilt,
I wake
from my delirium.
                        Tonight,
you're out of town,
asleep in some hotel
half a continent away.
You haven't robbed me
of the covers
that keep me warm and snug.
And I'm still as comfy as a cat
pressed against
a sunny windowpane.
                        Now,
instead of great art,
I am reminded
of the story
of the man
who complains
about his itching toes
after
his leg's
been amputated at the knee.

III.

But, unlike my friend
who'll never scratch
his toes again,
I know
that you'll be home
in two more nights.
And maybe, after
we disconnect our loins
and you fall asleep
upon your side,
you'll begin again
to wind those blankets 'round.

As

I turn my head back, relieved
that neither you
nor anyone else
has seen my foolishness,
I suddenly long
for the prickly touch
of cold night air
that comes
whenever my covers
slip away.

That's

because it comes with you,
who awes me
with the largeness
of your presence
even
in the midst
of your absence.

Finishing Touches

We lay sideways
under the sheltering
sheet. I
have wedged myself
against the back
of you, my arms
wrapped
around your sides,
my hands
around your breasts.
Your hands
cover mine.

We talk
in touches now.

We listen
to each other's fingertips.

About the Author

David Meuel's poems have been published in dozens of literary journals and magazines in both the United States and Canada. He has also received recognition in several poetry contests, most notably the Biennial Poetry Competition sponsored by the Villa Montalvo Center for the Arts in Saratoga, California.

As well as poems, Meuel has written stage plays and television documentaries. One of his plays, a full-length family drama called *The End of All That*, was produced to favorable reviews in Palo Alto, California. Another, *Deliverance and Destiny*, is a one-act drama about Allen Allensworth, an ex-slave who went on to found a Black Utopian community in the San Joaquin Valley. It was commissioned by the State of California as part of its "Living History" play series. Meuel's documentaries include an hour-long piece on theatre for KTEH-TV, Channel 54, a PBS affiliate in San Jose. The show received a Cindy Award from the Informational Film Producers of America.

A graduate of both the University of California, Davis, and the University of Michigan, Ann Arbor, Meuel works as a freelance writer and lives in Palo Alto with his wife, Barbara, and son, Jimmy.

Book Design and Typography: Hall Kelley
Type: Adobe Garamond Family
Printer: Oakmead Printing